Picture credits:
l: Left, r: Right, t: Top, b: Bottom, c: Center

13t: Leeman, 20t: GavinD, 22t: Michael John Kielty/CORBIS, 26t: Nburka,
28t: Harvey Fitzhugh, 28b: Andrew Barker, 32-33C: British Library,
34t: Charles Taylor, 34b: James Glover,
37t: Science Photo Library, 38t: Hazeelin Hassan,
40-41t: Elena Ray, 40b: stevephotos,

Copyright: Really Useful Map Company (HK) Ltd.
Published By: Robert Frederick Ltd.
4 North Parade Bath, England.

First Published: 2006

Henry VIII

CONTENTS

Tudor Rule

England was torn by a civil war between 1455 and 1485. This conflict was known as the War of the Roses, and involved the royal houses of Lancaster and York. Both wanted to rule England. At first the House of Lancaster gained control. Later, in 1461, Edward, the Duke of York ascended the throne as King Edward IV.

The tale of two princes

When Edward IV died, his son Edward V was supposed to become the king. However, later Richard III, the younger brother of Edward IV wanted the throne for himself. Therefore, he spread the rumour that evil people were trying to kill Edward V and his younger brother. He made the two princes stay at the Tower of London and began to rule England on the behalf of Edward V. Later, Richard produced documents claiming that the marriage of Edward IV was illegal and therefore, Edward V did not have a right to become king. Instead, Richard made himself the new king of England.

Peace, at last!

Richard was a cruel king, and soon his people began to get tired of his rule. It was during this time that Henry Tudor, a Lancastrian, decided to try and gain control of England. On August 22, 1485 Henry defeated King Richard at the Battle of Bosworth Field. Richard was killed in the battle and Henry was crowned the new king of England marking the beginning of the Tudor rule.

❤ *It is believed that the cruel Richard III had his young nephews killed while they were imprisoned in the Tower of London*

HENRY VII•(January 28, 1457 - April 21, 1509)•October 30, 1485 – Coronation
•January 18, 1486 – Married Elizabeth of York•June 28, 1491 – Birth of Henry VIII

6 7

Birth of Henry VIII

As soon as he came to power, Henry VII came up with a plan to end the long fight between the Lancastrians and the Yorkists. He married Elizabeth, the eldest daughter of Edward IV uniting the two houses and founding a new one – the House of Tudor. Henry VII and Elizabeth had seven children, of whom three died very young. Arthur, the Prince of Wales was the eldest. He was followed by Margaret, Henry the future king of England and Mary.

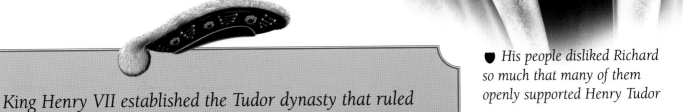

● His people disliked Richard so much that many of them openly supported Henry Tudor

● The "queen" in playing cards is believed to have been modelled after Elizabeth York, the mother of Henry VIII

King Henry VII established the Tudor dynasty that ruled England for over a hundred years from 1485. His rule also marked the end of a period of unrest in England. The thirty-year old civil war that had ravaged the country was replaced by a relatively peaceful era. Although Henry VII was a clever and efficient king, his position was always in danger. Many plots were made to replace him. Henry VII however managed to survive, by making peace with his neighbouring countries so that the conspirators would not get any foreign aid. He entered into a treaty with France and also made trade agreement with the Netherlands. He also arranged the marriage of his eldest son, Arthur with Catharine, the daughter of the king of Spain. Under the rule of Henry VII, England once again became a powerful country with a strong economy.

Henry VIII was born at Greenwich on June 28, 1491. He had an elder brother, Arthur and an elder sister, Margaret. Arthur was given more importance than Henry, by their father King Henry VII as the heir to the throne of England.

A sheltered life

Most of Henry's childhood was spent with his mother. Young Henry led a sheltered life, as his mother was very protective. His father spent much of his time grooming Arthur for his role as the future king. When Arthur died the king was heart broken. Despite Henry being the next in line of succession, the king did not show the same interest in him as he had in Arthur. This made the father and son grow even more distant.

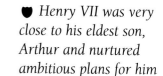

● Henry VII was very close to his eldest son, Arthur and nurtured ambitious plans for him

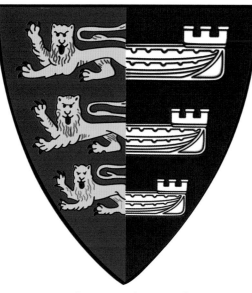

● The Coat of Arms of the Cinque Ports is one of the oldest known heraldic emblems of England

Titles galore

Being the second son of King Henry VII, Henry was created the Duke of York. This title had become extinct when Richard the second son of King Edward IV and the brother of Edward V died without heirs. The title was revived when Henry was born. Henry was also made the Lord Warden of the Cinque Ports when he was just two years old. The Lord Warden of the Cinque Ports was in charge of the five port towns in the southern coast of England. When his brother, Arthur died in April 2, 1502, Henry inherited the title of Prince of Wales and also became the heir to the throne of England.

A marriage agreement

Henry was only ten years old when he attended his brother's wedding. Arthur married the Spanish princess, Catherine of Aragon in November 1501. A few months later, Arthur died. Henry VII sought the Pope's permission to marry his second son to Catherine. Although, the Pope gave permission, the king seemed to lose interest in the alliance. Therefore, the marriage did not take place until Henry VIII came to power.

Catherine refused to accept her divorce, until her death. She even signed her last letter, "Catherine the Queen"

Catherine was the youngest daughter of King Ferdinand II of Aragon and his wife Isabella I of Castille. She was also the great-granddaughter of King Edward III of England and was therefore the cousin of Henry VII. Catherine was only 16 when she married Prince Arthur. A few months later both Catherine and her husband fell seriously ill. Catherine recovered from the illness, only to find out that her husband had died. She was then promised to the next heir – Henry VIII. The marriage did not take place until Henry came to power. The couple seemed happy enough for about 18 years. Catherine even gave birth to a daughter, Mary. However, Henry wanted a male heir and he began to look for excuses to marry another woman. Finally, in 1531 Henry divorced Catherine and married Anne Boleyn.

Henry VII died on April 21, 1509. He was succeeded by his younger son, Henry the Prince of Wales. Henry VIII was crowned the king of England on June 24, 1509 a few days after his marriage to Catherine of Aragon. William Warham, the Archbishop of Canterbury presided over both the marriage and the coronation.

Striving to be different

Henry's relationship with his father influenced his decisions a great deal. The ambitious young king wanted to prove to himself and his country that he was a better monarch. Therefore, he reversed many of his father's policies the moment he came to power. Henry also executed several trusted servants of Henry VII and did not show any mercy to his enemies. Henry VIII soon proved to be the exact opposite of his peace-loving father.

An athletic monarch

In his younger days, King Henry VIII was tall and athletic. He was nothing like the overweight monarch we now remember. He loved to joust and hunt, and was known to tire at least eight horses a day. The young king was also very fond of tennis. He loved dancing and often took part in wrestling bouts. Henry also had a huge appetite and relished good food.

WILLIAM WARHAM • *(c. 1450-August 22, 1532)* • *1502 – Became Bishop of London and Keeper of the Great Seal* • *1504- Became Lord Chancellor and Archbishop of Canterbury*

10 11

A learned king

● *Henry VIII being crowned the king of England by William Warham, the Archbishop of Canterbury at the time*

Henry was as intelligent as he was athletic. He spoke French, Latin and Spanish fluently and loved to read. He had a deep knowledge of shipping and was well versed in mathematics and astronomy. Henry was also very religious and attended three masses a day. He loved music and even composed many pieces. At the same time, the young king was fond of gambling and was known to lose large amounts of money on cards.

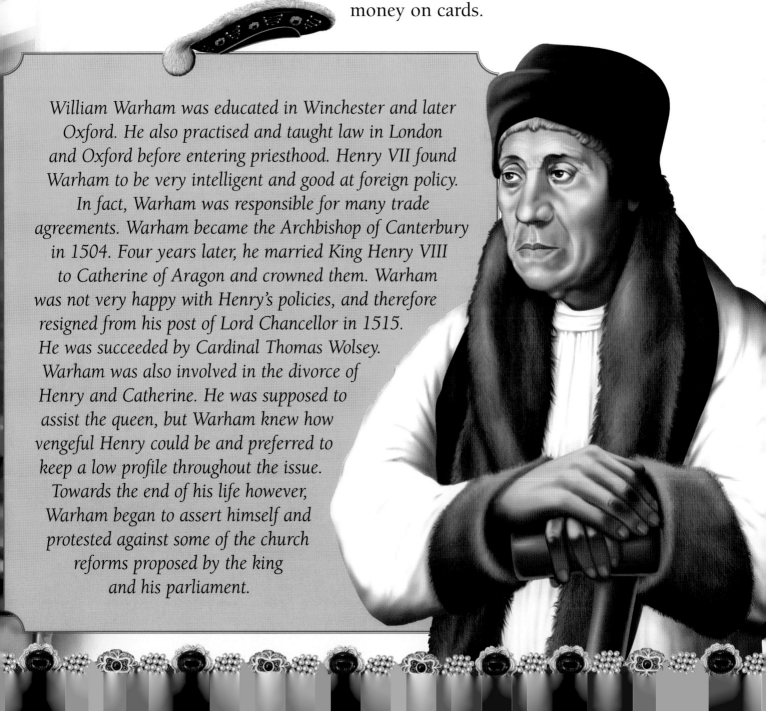

William Warham was educated in Winchester and later Oxford. He also practised and taught law in London and Oxford before entering priesthood. Henry VII found Warham to be very intelligent and good at foreign policy. In fact, Warham was responsible for many trade agreements. Warham became the Archbishop of Canterbury in 1504. Four years later, he married King Henry VIII to Catherine of Aragon and crowned them. Warham was not very happy with Henry's policies, and therefore resigned from his post of Lord Chancellor in 1515. He was succeeded by Cardinal Thomas Wolsey. Warham was also involved in the divorce of Henry and Catherine. He was supposed to assist the queen, but Warham knew how vengeful Henry could be and preferred to keep a low profile throughout the issue. Towards the end of his life however, Warham began to assert himself and protested against some of the church reforms proposed by the king and his parliament.

Unlike his father, Henry VIII liked to wage wars. He spent a huge amount of money in wars and in fortifying the boundaries of England. Throughout his rule Henry made many unsuccessful attempts to conquer Scotland and France.

The Holy League

In 1511, Henry joined the Holy League against the French king, Louis XII. Henry's father-in-law, Ferdinand II and the Holy Roman Emperor, Maximilian I were also a part of this league. Henry also signed the Treaty of Westminster, with Ferdinand II, under which the two agreed to support each other against France.

Trouble at home

In the next few months after their alliance, the Holy League won many battles. Henry especially proved to be very successful. In a desperate attempt to distract Henry, Louis XII encouraged King James IV of Scotland to invade England at this time. The Scottish king arrived at Flodden with an army of about 60,000 men. The English, led by Thomas Howard, the Earl of Surrey, had a much smaller army, yet the Scots suffered one of their worst defeats in history at the Battle of Flodden Field.

🕮 The pink region in the map represents the countries that were a part of the Holy League

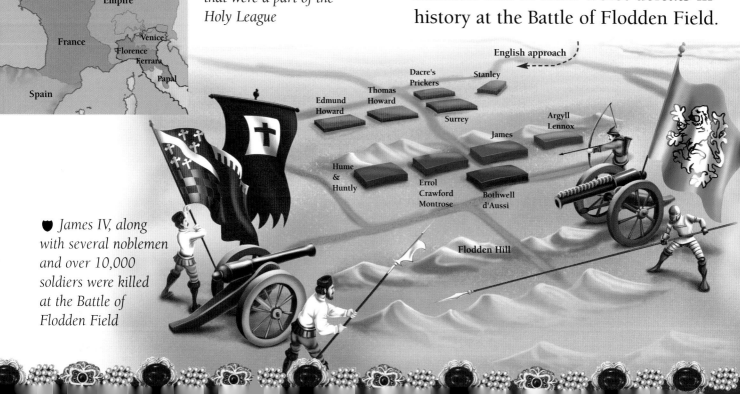

🕮 James IV, along with several noblemen and over 10,000 soldiers were killed at the Battle of Flodden Field

POPE JULIUS II•(*December 5, 1443-February 21, 1513*)•*1471 – Became Bishop of Carpentras, France*•*1471 – Made Cardinal of San Pietor and Vincula*•*1503 – Elected Pope*

12 13

● *Julius was responsible for laying the foundation of the new St. Peter's Basilica*

The fall of the League

Ferdinand left the League in 1514, and Henry was forced to make peace with Louis XII. When Louis XII died, his son-in-law Francis I came to power. Francis immediately set out to regain control of Italy. He defeated what was left of the Holy League at the Battle of Marignano. He also made peace with Charles V, the new king of Spain. The Holy Roman Emperor, Maximilian I also entered into a treaty with Francis. By the end of 1516, the war over Italy had ended.

Known as the "warrior pope", Julius II was a nephew of Pope Sixtus IV. During the papacy of Sixtus, Julius became very powerful. Pope Sixtus IV was succeeded by Pope Innocent VIII in 1484. It was thought that Julius would be the next pope. However, Cardinal Rodrigo Borgia succeeded Pope Innocent VIII instead. Borgia died in 1503, and Julius became pope. As pope, Julius formed first, the League of Cambrai against the Venetians and then the Holy League against France to gain control of Italy. Although his achievements were mainly political and military, Julius II also contributed to the development of art and literature. It was he who commissioned Michelangelo to paint the ceiling of the Sistine Chapel. Julius was succeeded by Pope Leo X.

The Field of Cloth of Gold

The peace following the War of the Holy League did not last long. The enmity between France and Spain was re-ignited after the death of Maximilian I in 1519. Both Francis I and Charles V wanted to become the next Holy Roman Emperor. Eventually, Charles V was preferred as he was Maximilian's grandson.

Field of Cloth of Gold

🖤 *The map shows the Field of Cloth of Gold where Henry VIII met King Francis I*

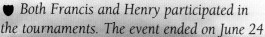

🖤 *Both Francis and Henry participated in the tournaments. The event ended on June 24*

Courting England

France, Spain and England signed the Treaty of London in 1518, agreeing to aid each other in case of foreign attacks. When Maximilian died, the situation changed. Charles V became the Holy Roman Emperor, and the enmity between Spain and France grew. Both Francis and Charles began to compete for Henry's support. The English king met Charles V in the Netherlands and later, at Calais, France. Francis did not want to be outdone and so he arranged a grand meeting with Henry at a valley in Balinghem, near Calais.

A grand affair

Magnificent tents, extravagant feasts and jousting events were just some of the highlights of the meeting. The tents and clothes were made from expensive fabric woven with silk and gold thread giving the meeting place its name – Le Camp de Drap d'Or, or the Field of Cloth of Gold. A spectacular temporary palace was built for Henry at the site. Francis and Henry met on June 7, 1520. This was followed by over two weeks of tournaments and banquets.

FRANCIS I • *(September 12, 1494-July 31, 1547)* • *1515 – Crowned king of France*
• *1524 – Financed Giovanni da Verrazano's expedition to North America*

14 15

Enemies again

The meeting was one of the most talked about events in Europe at the time. However, it failed to achieve its goal – bring France and England together against Charles V. According to some accounts, Henry lost a wrestling match to Francis. This annoyed the English king a great deal and he refused to consider friendship with France. Whatever the reasons, the relations between England and France worsened after the meeting, and Henry allied with Charles. Following this, the Holy Roman Emperor declared war against France in 1521.

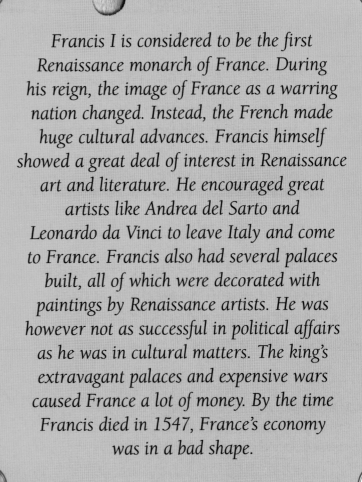

Francis I is considered to be the first Renaissance monarch of France. During his reign, the image of France as a warring nation changed. Instead, the French made huge cultural advances. Francis himself showed a great deal of interest in Renaissance art and literature. He encouraged great artists like Andrea del Sarto and Leonardo da Vinci to leave Italy and come to France. Francis also had several palaces built, all of which were decorated with paintings by Renaissance artists. He was however not as successful in political affairs as he was in cultural matters. The king's extravagant palaces and expensive wars caused France a lot of money. By the time Francis died in 1547, France's economy was in a bad shape.

Foreign Affairs

After losing the crown of the Holy Roman Emperor to Charles V, Francis decided to invade the latter's territory. He was supported by the Republic of Venice and a number of smaller Italian states. Meanwhile, Charles V formed an alliance with Henry VIII, and the Italian War of 1521 began.

Initial battles

Henry saw the battle between the Holy Roman Emperor and Francis as a golden opportunity to strengthen England's position in Europe. He therefore offered Charles V complete support in the ensuing battles. In the beginning, the French made considerable advances into the Habsburg territory. They even seized many key cities. At the Battle of Pampeluna, the French seemed to be heading for victory when Charles V himself got involved in the conflict. This made the French forces withdraw. In Italy, the French tried to re-capture Milan, which they had lost to Spain in November 1521. They were supported by the Venetians and Swiss mercenaries, but were eventually defeated by the stronger Spanish army.

 The blue line depicts the movement of the French army, and the red shows Spanish movement during the Battle of Pavia

Battle of Pavia

As the French began to lose ground, many of its allies joined Charles V. With the help of these allies and the English, Charles managed to defeat the French at the Battle of Pavia. He also captured Francis during this battle. When Henry heard the news he planned an invasion of France. However, the invasion did not take place for lack of funds. Furthermore, Charles V, who had promised Henry his help in the invasion, opted out leaving Henry with no choice but to abandon his plans.

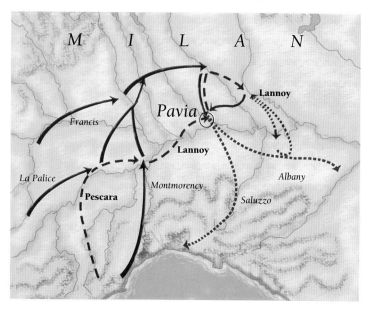

POPE LEO X•*(December 11, 1475-December 1, 1521)•1March 26, 1492 – Became a cardinal*
•*March 9, 1513 – Became Pope•January 3, 1521 – Excommunicated Martin Luther*

16   17

Defending the faith

Apart from his involvement in the power struggle in Europe, Henry VIII also played a major role in the religious affairs of the continent. He wrote the *Defence of the Seven Sacraments*, criticising the German monk, Martin Luther's attack on Catholicism. The book was dedicated to Pope Leo X. The Pope in turn gave Henry the title of *Fidei Defensor*, or "Defender of the Faith".

Martin Luther accused the Roman Catholic Church of corruption and began the Protestant movement in Europe

Pope Leo X was the son of Lorenzo di Piero de'Medici, an Italian politician. Leo was only 16 when he became a cardinal and moved to Rome. However, his father died soon after leaving Italy open to a series of foreign invasion. The Medici family were forced to leave Florence by invading French forces. Leo managed to find refuge in Bologna. He then began to travel to other parts of Europe for sometime before finally returning to Rome. He however kept away from public life and pursued his literary interests. As pope, Leo supported many charities including hospitals and shelter for wounded soldiers and pilgrims. He was however, unable to prevent the Protestant Reformation that started during his term. In fact, Martin Luther first accused the Roman Catholic Church of corruption during Leo's time. The Pope reacted by excommunicating Luther.

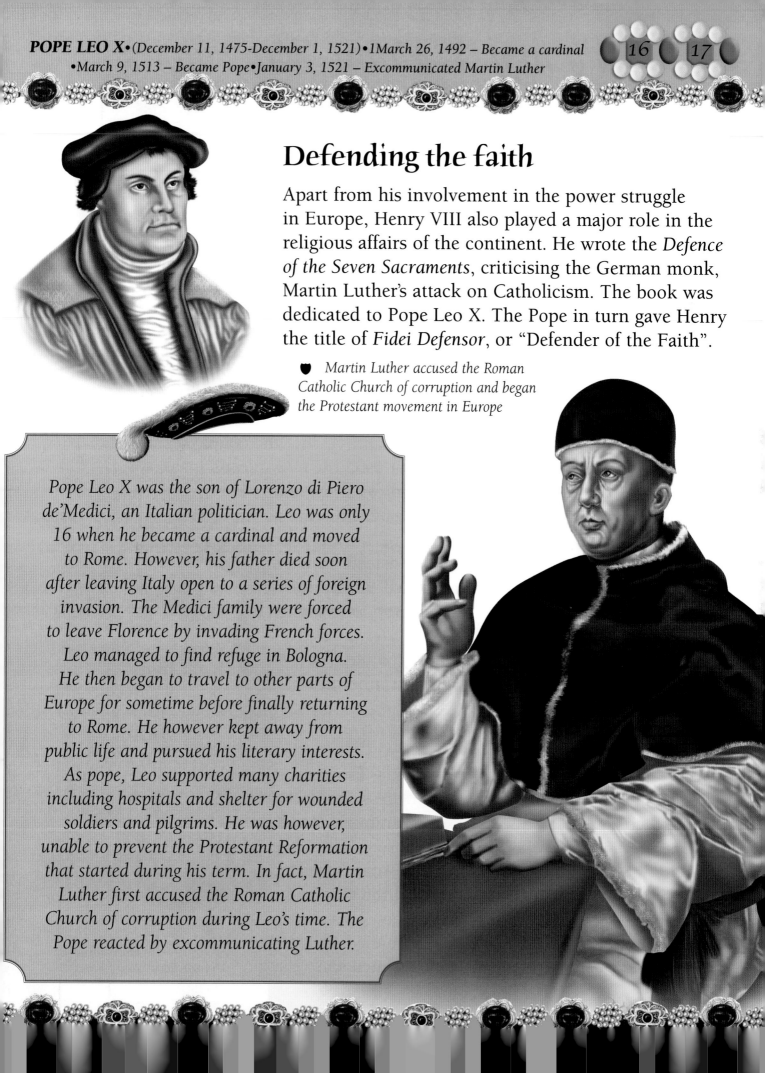

Henry's Many Marriages

"Divorced, beheaded, died, divorced, beheaded, survived." – that was the fate of the six wives of King Henry VIII. So, why did the king get married six times? He was driven by the desire for a son who would take over the throne of England after he died.

♥ Henry's many marriages caused a religious turmoil in England that finally led to the break between the Roman Catholic Church and the Church of England

A religious struggle

Henry wedded his first wife, Catherine of Aragon in 1509, just nine weeks after becoming the king of England. At first the couple seemed very happy, but soon the new queen's inability to have a son drove them apart. Henry sought permission from the pope to divorce Catherine and marry Anne Boleyn instead. However, the pope denied him permission. This did not stop Henry who married Anne anyway and had her declared the Queen of England in Catherine's place.

Trouble in paradise

Queen Anne gave birth to only one child – Princess Elizabeth. Henry made Elizabeth his heiress and declared Catherine's daughter Princess Mary illegitimate. However, when Queen Anne also failed to have a son, Henry began to get impatient. Finally, he had Queen Anne beheaded on charges of witchcraft, plotting to kill the king and having relationships with other men. Soon after Anne's death Henry married Jane Seymour, who died after giving birth to Prince Edward, Henry's long-awaited son.

♥ Anne Boleyn was beheaded on false charges of witchcraft and treachery

KATHERINE PARR•1527 – Married Lord Edward Borough•1529 – Lord Borough died and Katherine married John Neville•1543 – Married King Henry VIII•1547 – Henry VIII died

18 19

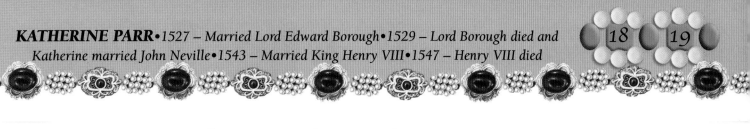

The search continues...

Henry was thrilled to finally have an heir, but he was worried about his son's health. Prince Edward was very weak and often fell ill. Henry realised that Edward was too weak to rule the country efficiently. The king decided to marry once again to ensure a healthy heir to the throne. His short marriage to Anne of Cleves ended in a divorce. Henry then married Catherine Howard, who was Anne Boleyn's cousin. However, hardly two years later, Catherine Howard was beheaded for having relationships with two other men. In 1543, Henry married his last wife, Katherine Parr. Henry's dream of having another son remained just that – a dream.

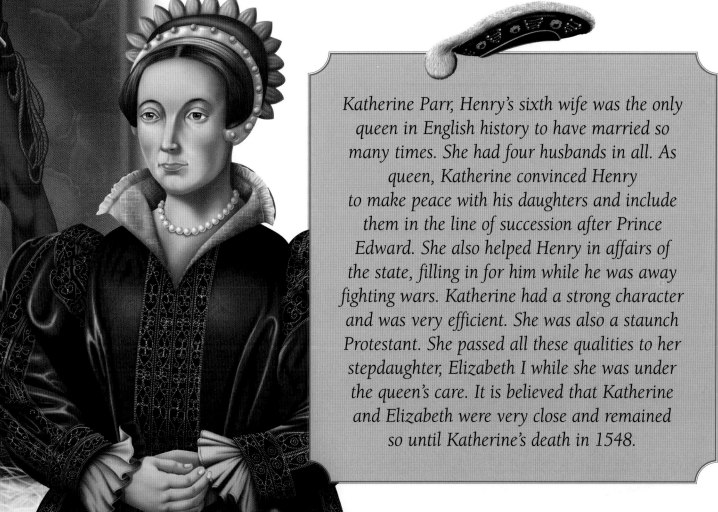

Katherine Parr, Henry's sixth wife was the only queen in English history to have married so many times. She had four husbands in all. As queen, Katherine convinced Henry to make peace with his daughters and include them in the line of succession after Prince Edward. She also helped Henry in affairs of the state, filling in for him while he was away fighting wars. Katherine had a strong character and was very efficient. She was also a staunch Protestant. She passed all these qualities to her stepdaughter, Elizabeth I while she was under the queen's care. It is believed that Katherine and Elizabeth were very close and remained so until Katherine's death in 1548.

Cardinal Thomas Wolsey was the true power behind the throne of England. As a priest, Cardinal Wolsey was one of the most powerful clergymen in history. He was also a great politician who masterminded some of the major events in Europe at the time.

The rise of Wolsey

Wolsey was born into a poor family. He worked hard to pursue his studies at Oxford and enter the Church. In 1507, Wolsey became chaplain to Henry VII. Later, when his son Henry VIII came to power, Wolsey became the young king's guide and advisor. Henry VIII was happy to leave the main decisions to Wolsey as he was very efficient and trustworthy. Wolsey soon became Bishop of London, Archbishop of York and was finally made cardinal in 1515. He was also made a privy councillor and in 1515, given the position of the Lord Chancellor.

Foreign affairs

Wolsey showed a great deal of interest in foreign affairs. Throughout his term, Wolsey tried to promote England and make it a dominant European power. He supported Henry VIII and put forth his name as the next Holy Roman Emperor after Maximilian I. He also played a major role in organising the meeting at the Field of Cloth of Gold and later, persuading Henry to ally with Charles V against the French. Wolsey's tactics were aimed at maintaining England's advantage as a powerful ally that both France and Spain needed.

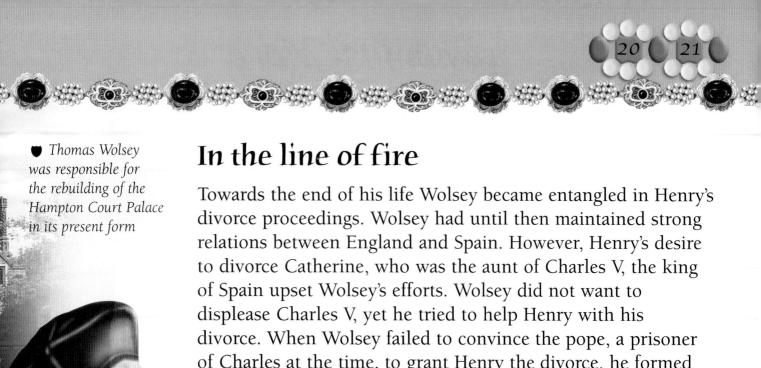

Thomas Wolsey was responsible for the rebuilding of the Hampton Court Palace in its present form

In the line of fire

Towards the end of his life Wolsey became entangled in Henry's divorce proceedings. Wolsey had until then maintained strong relations between England and Spain. However, Henry's desire to divorce Catherine, who was the aunt of Charles V, the king of Spain upset Wolsey's efforts. Wolsey did not want to displease Charles V, yet he tried to help Henry with his divorce. When Wolsey failed to convince the pope, a prisoner of Charles at the time, to grant Henry the divorce, he formed an alliance with France against Charles in order to free the pope. This attempt failed when France made peace with Spain. The impatient Henry charged Wolsey with high treason. However, Wolsey died on the way to his trial.

c. March 1471-75: Born in Ipswich, Suffolk
1509: Made Royal Secretary
1511: Made member of the Privy Council
1507: Becomes court chaplain to Henry VII
1514: Created Archbishop of York
1515: Created cardinal and appointed
as the Lord Chancellor of England
1520: Organises the meeting at
the Field of Cloth of Gold
1523: Made Prince-Bishop of Durham
November 4, 1530: Arrested at Cawood
Castle, Selby, near York on charges
of high treason
November 29, 1530: Dies
on the way to his trial

Thomas More was one of the most distinguished men to serve in the court of Henry VIII. He was trained under Cardinal Wolsey and was his loyal supporter. More took over from Wolsey as the Chancellor of England when the latter fell out of favour with the king.

Early life

More was the son of a judge in London. Even as a boy More felt that he was meant to be a priest. He therefore began his training under John Morton, the Archbishop of Canterbury at the time. In 1492, More left the Archbishop's household to continue his studies at Oxford. In 1504, he entered the House of Commons and became noticed for his powerful speeches. The king made him a member of the Privy Council and began to rely on him for advice. More proved very valuable during diplomatic missions.

● *Thomas More spent his initial years at Lambeth Palace, the residence of the Archbishop of Canterbury*

A difficult position

In 1529, More's guide and teacher, Wolsey was removed from office. More was at first not ready to replace Wolsey as he did not want to get involved in the king's divorce battle. Henry, however, promised More that he would not have to get involved. However, More was forced to help the king in every manner possible. Like Wolsey, More too did not succeed in the matter. It was then that Thomas Cromwell, the Secretary of the State at the time came up with a solution. More did not agree with Cromwell and therefore chose to resign and retire to his home in Chelsea.

February 7, 1478: Born in Milk Street, London
1492: Enters Oxford
1494: Studies law at the Inns of Court
1499: Completes his studies to become a lawyer
1504: Becomes a member of the parliament
1505: Marries Jane Colt
1515: Goes to Antwerp on a diplomatic mission. Begins writing his famous book, Utopia
1518: Appointed member of Privy Council
1523: Elected speaker of the Parliament
1529: Replaces Wolsey as Lord Chancellor
1532: Resigns from his post
1534: Sent to the Tower of London for refusing to accept the King as the Supreme Head of the Church
July 6, 1535: Beheaded after trial
1935: Declared a saint by Pope Pius XI.

● *More was beatified in 1886 by Pope Leo XIII and canonised in 1935. His feast day is on June 22*

A saintly end

More was not happy with the break with Rome. He maintained that although the Parliament had the right to declare Anne as queen, it held no religious authority. He declared that he would always regard the pope as the Head of the Church. More was imprisoned in the Tower of London for several days. Finally, he was charged with high treason and sentenced to death.

Henry and the Pope

Henry VIII had a long conflict with the Roman Catholic Church. Although the English king was a devout Catholic for most of his life, he defied papal authority whenever it judged against him, particularly where his marriages were concerned.

The beginning

When Catherine of Aragon failed to produce a male heir, Henry decided to divorce her and marry Anne Boleyn, whom he had become attracted to. At first, Henry ordered Cardinal Wolsey and William Warham to find some excuse to declare his marriage to Catherine illegal. When this plan failed, Henry approached Pope Clement VII. He sent his secretary William Knight to Rome. He told Knight to convince Pope Clement VII that Pope Julius II had been tricked into allowing Catherine to marry Henry.

Pope refuses

When Catherine found out about her husband's plan, she approached her nephew, Charles V the Holy Roman Emperor for help. Charles V told the pope not to grant Henry his wish. The pope did not want to displease either of the rulers. He therefore did as Charles told him to, but at the same time gave Henry permission to marry any woman. The pope thought that as he had not allowed the divorce, Henry would not be able to marry another woman.

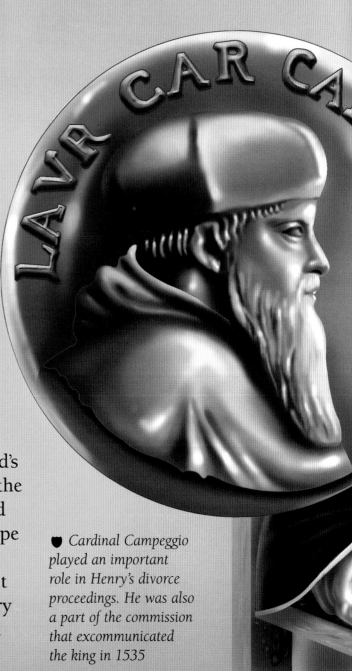

● *Cardinal Campeggio played an important role in Henry's divorce proceedings. He was also a part of the commission that excommunicated the king in 1535*

POPE CLEMENT VII • (May 26, 1478-September 25, 1534)
•September 28, 1513 – Became a cardinal •November 19, 1523 – Became pope

24 25

Henry defies the Pope

Cardinal Wolsey once again appealed to the pope on behalf of the king.
The pope finally agreed to look into Catherine's marriage to Henry.
He sent Lorenzo Cardinal Campeggio to England to investigate the
papal bull. The pope also instructed Cardinal Campeggio to declare
the bull illegal if the reasons for allowing the marriage were false.
However, the investigations were stopped after Charles V forced the pope
to recall Cardinal Campeggio. Henry became furious and decided to marry
Anne without the pope's permission.

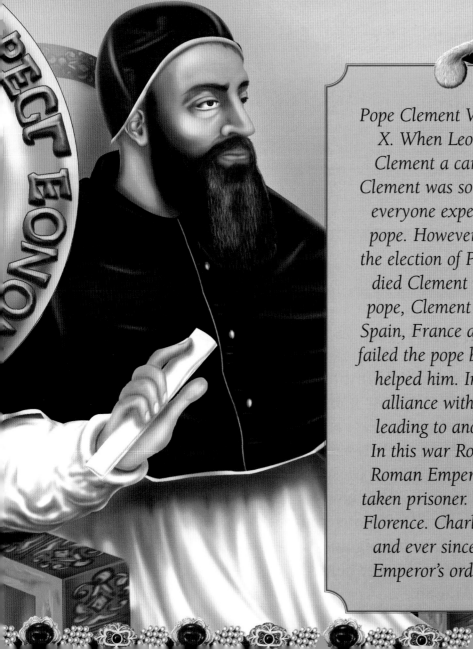

*Pope Clement VII was the cousin of Pope Leo
X. When Leo became the pope, he made
Clement a cardinal and his main advisor.
Clement was so involved in papal affairs that
everyone expected him to become the next
pope. However, Clement himself supported
the election of Pope Adrian VI. When Adrian
died Clement was elected the pope. As the
pope, Clement tried to bring peace between
Spain, France and England. When his efforts
failed the pope began to support any side that
helped him. In 1526, the pope formed an
alliance with France against Charles V,
leading to another series of Italian Wars.
In this war Rome was sacked by The Holy
Roman Emperor's forces and the pope was
taken prisoner. His family was expelled from
Florence. Charles V later restored his power,
and ever since Pope Clement followed the
Emperor's orders, until his death in 1534.*

Henry's decision to marry Anne Boleyn without papal permission was due to the fact that Anne was pregnant. Henry, who hoped for a male heir, did not want the child to be declared illegal. He therefore made arrangements for the marriage.

A secret wedding

Henry married Anne in a secret ceremony on January 25, 1533. Thomas Cranmer who was at the wedding was later appointed the Archbishop of Canterbury following William Warham's death. Henry had chosen Cranmer as he believed that Cranmer would support his policies. Just as the king had expected, Cranmer declared his marriage to Catherine invalid and Anne his legal wife.

● Henry's desire to marry Anne Boleyn was responsible for the establishment of an independant Church of England

Henry's excommunication

The pope was furious at the developments in England. He immediately excommunicated Henry for going against the Roman Catholic Church. The English Parliament responded by passing a series of laws to distance the Church of England from Rome. The first of these laws was the Statute in Restraint of Appeals. This law prevented people from consulting the pope in all religious matters. The king's word was final and anyone in England who appealed to the pope was punished. This act helped Henry to divorce Catherine of Aragon.

Other religious acts

The Parliament passed several other laws, all of which eventually contributed to the formation of the Anglican Church. One of these acts required the election of bishops nominated by the king. The Act of Supremacy of 1534 declared that the king was the Supreme head of the Church of England. The Treasons Act of 1534 declared that anyone who refused to accept the king as the Supreme Head would be punished by death.

The Act of Succession of 1534 declared Mary, Henry's daughter by Catherine of Aragon as illegal

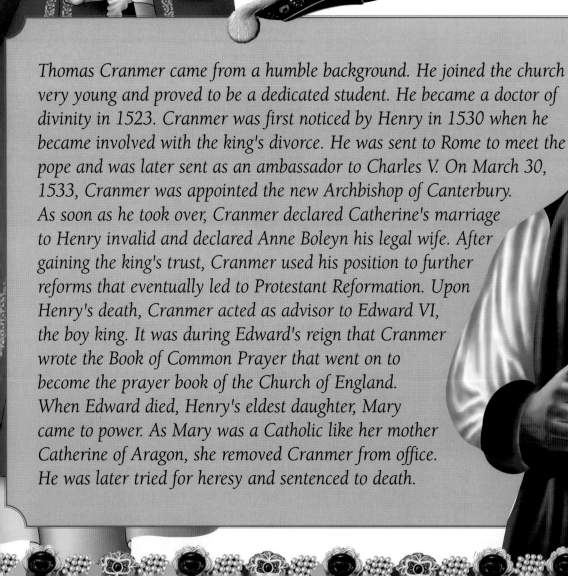

Thomas Cranmer came from a humble background. He joined the church very young and proved to be a dedicated student. He became a doctor of divinity in 1523. Cranmer was first noticed by Henry in 1530 when he became involved with the king's divorce. He was sent to Rome to meet the pope and was later sent as an ambassador to Charles V. On March 30, 1533, Cranmer was appointed the new Archbishop of Canterbury. As soon as he took over, Cranmer declared Catherine's marriage to Henry invalid and declared Anne Boleyn his legal wife. After gaining the king's trust, Cranmer used his position to further reforms that eventually led to Protestant Reformation. Upon Henry's death, Cranmer acted as advisor to Edward VI, the boy king. It was during Edward's reign that Cranmer wrote the Book of Common Prayer that went on to become the prayer book of the Church of England. When Edward died, Henry's eldest daughter, Mary came to power. As Mary was a Catholic like her mother Catherine of Aragon, she removed Cranmer from office. He was later tried for heresy and sentenced to death.

Dissolution of Monasteries

The Act of Supremacy gave the king a huge amount of authority over religious matters in England. Under this act, the king could also seize the property of monasteries attached to the Catholic Church. Henry used his authority and started to dissolve the monasteries.

Minor changes

The Anglican Church retained most of the Catholic traditions. However, certain minor changes were made to reform the church. The Parliament passed acts to control corruption in the church. These acts limited the amount of money charged for services like burying the dead in the Church cemetery and reduced the number of church offices that could be held by one man. In 1534, Henry gave Thomas Cromwell instructions to visit the monasteries and make sure they were following the rules.

The dissolution

The actual reason Henry sent Cromwell and his men to the monasteries was to make a list of all their property. The Church was far richer than the State. Henry wanted to use its wealth to clear his debts. The visitors returned with reports of corruption and malpractices. The people were told that the monks and nuns were using their money to live luxuriously, and that if the king got the property of the monasteries, he would never have to tax the people again. By 1536, monasteries were being seized.

The Fountains Abbey in Yorkshire were one of the monasteries to be exploited during the dissolution

The aftermath

● *Worcester Cathedral had about 600 books before the dissolution. Today, only six of them remain intact*

The abbots who resisted the king's move were put to death. Following this, most abbots signed their monasteries over to the king. Some of the buildings were destroyed completely, while smaller ones were bought by parishes. Some of the abbeys were even sold to individuals. The abbeys were centres of learning and sources of charity and medical care. Most of the libraries attached to monasteries were destroyed. Books were sold for their valuable binding, or destroyed . There were a few protests against the king. Henry suppressed these revolts and executed the leaders of such uprisings.

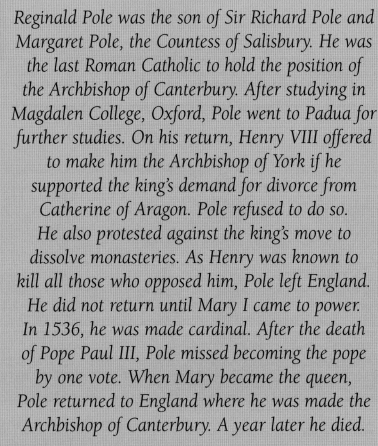

Reginald Pole was the son of Sir Richard Pole and Margaret Pole, the Countess of Salisbury. He was the last Roman Catholic to hold the position of the Archbishop of Canterbury. After studying in Magdalen College, Oxford, Pole went to Padua for further studies. On his return, Henry VIII offered to make him the Archbishop of York if he supported the king's demand for divorce from Catherine of Aragon. Pole refused to do so. He also protested against the king's move to dissolve monasteries. As Henry was known to kill all those who opposed him, Pole left England. He did not return until Mary I came to power. In 1536, he was made cardinal. After the death of Pope Paul III, Pole missed becoming the pope by one vote. When Mary became the queen, Pole returned to England where he was made the Archbishop of Canterbury. A year later he died.

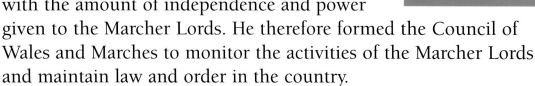

The acts that severed the ties between the Church of England and Rome were not the only laws passed by the Parliament during Henry's reign. A series of other acts were also enacted during Henry's time. The most significant of these acts was the Laws in Wales Acts that united England and Wales.

An unruly nation

Under the Statute of Rhuddlan of 1284, Wales was divided into five major counties. Although these counties followed the English common law, Welsh law continued to be used in many cases, until Henry VII became king of England. Although Henry VII did not make any change to the system of governing, he was not happy with the amount of independence and power given to the Marcher Lords. He therefore formed the Council of Wales and Marches to monitor the activities of the Marcher Lords and maintain law and order in the country.

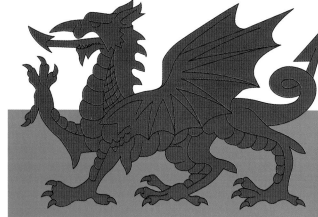

The flag of Wales

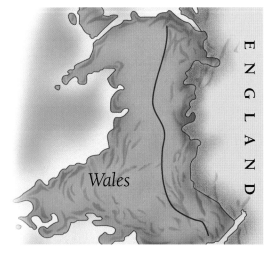

A map of Wales showing the Welsh Marches, which were once governed by Marcher Lords

The union of Wales

Like his father, Henry VIII did not want to make any changes to the Welsh government in the beginning. The power and number of the Marcher Lords had also reduced by the time Henry came to power. However, the remaining Marcher Lords soon began to pose a threat. Henry therefore told Thomas Cromwell to find a solution. Cromwell advised the king to unite Wales with England thereby bringing both countries under the same law and administration. This was done through the Laws in Wales Acts of 1535-1542.

THOMAS CROMWELL • (c. 1485-July 28, 1540) • 1523 – Became Member of Parliament
• 1533 – Appointed Secretary of State • 1557 – Made Archbishop of Canterbury

30 31

A dramatic change

One of the major changes caused by the acts was the introduction of a law and justice system in Wales that was the same as England. New counties were created in Wales to make administration easier. Marcher lordships were eliminated and the courts of Marcher Lords were banned from trying criminal cases. The borders of Wales were established and the country was also allowed to elect representatives into the English Parliament.

Thomas Cromwell was born into a middle class family. He worked under Cardinal Thomas Wolsey, until the latter became unpopular with the king. Cromwell took advantage of the situation and gained the king's trust. Within a few years, Henry made Cromwell his Secretary of State. Cromwell was the main force behind the formation of the Church of England. Being a Protestant himself, Cromwell urged the king to make several religious reforms and was involved in the dissolution of monasteries. Cromwell also played a major role in the king's personal life. He helped Henry get rid of Anne Boleyn and marry Jane Seymour. When Queen Jane died soon after giving birth to Prince Edward, Cromwell encouraged the king to marry Anne of Cleves. Henry was however disappointed with his new wife, and was furious with Cromwell for making him marry her. He was executed for this offence on July 28, 1540.

Henry VIII was a ruthless monarch. At the same time he was a great patron of arts, especially music. Henry wrote poems, songs and played many musical instruments. He also encouraged architecture, although he did not do much for visual arts like painting and sculpture, unlike his French counterpart, Francis I.

Musical monarch

Music was Henry's passion. He could sing well and play an assortment of instruments including the lute. The king also wrote several pieces of music, the most well-known being *Pastyme with Good Company*. Henry employed over 50 musicians in his court. He also expected his wives and children to share his passion for music. In fact, it is believed that Henry was attracted to Anne Boleyn mainly due to her ability to sing, dance and play musical instruments like the flute and the harp.

♥ *Henry had many portaits of himself painted during his lifetime*

The visual arts

Henry was not a great patron of paintings. However, he liked having his portrait made and therefore encouraged portrait artists to a great extent. He was the first English monarch to commission portraits of the royal family. He mainly employed foreign artists for the job, the most notable being Hans Holbein the Younger. Holbein not only painted the king's portraits but also designed his state robes. Other artists of the time included Levina Teerline and Hans Eworth.

HANS HOLBEIN, THE YOUNGER • (c. 1497-July 28, 1543) • 1526 – Arrives in London • 1527 – Paints the portrait of Sir Thomas More • 1543 – Dies from plague

32 33

Tudor architecture

● *Henry played several musical instruments including the harp and the lute*

The famous Tudor style of architecture that began during the reign of Henry VII continued to thrive under his son. Henry VIII had many new buildings constructed and improved upon several of the existing ones, including Hampton Court Palace, Christ Church at Oxford and the Palace of Whitehall. The architectural style of the time was greatly influenced by the ancient Gothic style. The four-centred arch, oriel windows, gables, turrets, small window panes, high roofs and large chimneys with decorative chimney pots are some of the distinctive features of Tudor architecture.

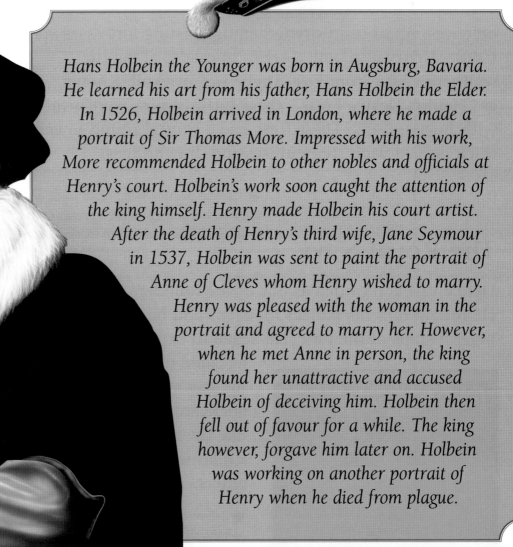

Hans Holbein the Younger was born in Augsburg, Bavaria. He learned his art from his father, Hans Holbein the Elder. In 1526, Holbein arrived in London, where he made a portrait of Sir Thomas More. Impressed with his work, More recommended Holbein to other nobles and officials at Henry's court. Holbein's work soon caught the attention of the king himself. Henry made Holbein his court artist. After the death of Henry's third wife, Jane Seymour in 1537, Holbein was sent to paint the portrait of Anne of Cleves whom Henry wished to marry. Henry was pleased with the woman in the portrait and agreed to marry her. However, when he met Anne in person, the king found her unattractive and accused Holbein of deceiving him. Holbein then fell out of favour for a while. The king however, forgave him later on. Holbein was working on another portrait of Henry when he died from plague.

Henry's rule was dominated by wars with other European powers. Henry's divorce from Catherine of Aragon and the resulting religious turmoil also put England in danger of invasions. Charles V openly threatened to attack England if Henry divorced his aunt and married Anne Boleyn. All this made Henry invest a great deal of money in building his armed forces.

The device forts

The threat of invasion from Spain made Henry strengthen his coastal defences. Apart from strengthening existing fortresses such as the Dover Castle, Henry also built a series of castles along the southern coast, from East Anglia to Cornwall. Known as "Henry's Device Forts", these fortifications were armed with huge canons. These forts had a central round tower, thick curved walls, portcullises and drawbridges.

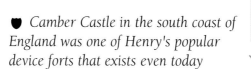

● *Camber Castle in the south coast of England was one of Henry's popular device forts that exists even today*

The Royal Navy

Henry VIII is regarded as one of the founders of the Royal Navy. He followed in his father's footsteps and built some of the biggest ships of the time. He began to expand the navy as soon as he came to power in preparation for the war against France. He built several dockyards and created new naval posts like the royal shipwright. He also established a marine organisation comprising seven officers headed by a Lieutenant.

● *Henry commissioned the Anthony Roll, which contained a survey of his navy. The record is now kept in the Pepys Library (pictured left)*

The Great Harry was one of the first ships to have gunports. This vessel had 43 heavy guns and over 140 light guns

The great ships

Henry built some of the biggest ships of the time. His naval vessels are often referred to as the "great ships". They included the famous *Mary Rose* and *Henri Grace a Dieu*, or *Great Harry*. Both ships were revolutionary in their design with gunports on the sides of the ships to facilitate firing from the sides instead of the front. *Great Harry* was the first English double-decker ship and the most powerful of all warships of the time. It is believed that Henry had this ship built to compete with the Scottish ship *Michael* that was launched in 1511.

Henry's Device Forts

Camber Castle – 1512
Walmer Castle – 1539-40
Deal Castle – 1539-40
Sandown Castle – 1539-40
Sandgate Castle – 1539
Southsea Castle - 1544
Hurst Castle - 1544
Calshot Castle – 1544
Yarmouth Castle – 1547
Portland Castle - 1539

The *Mary Rose* is the most enduring of all Tudor ships. The vessel was way ahead of its time and Henry VIII was extremely proud of her. It's believed that the king named the vessel after his beloved sister, Mary, and the Tudor rose.

First of its kind

The *Mary Rose* was unique in many ways. It was the largest ship of its time, until *Great Harry* was built. It was one of the first English ships to be built only for wartime use. Until then, merchant ships were converted for the purpose. The *Mary Rose* had about 78 guns aboard. Unlike most ships of the time this Tudor ship had gunports on its sides. The ship was about 38.5 m long and could carry a crew of over 400 men.

❤ Mary Rose *had an illustrious naval career, ever since its launch in 1509*

In service

The *Mary Rose* was Admiral Edward Howard's flagship during the Italian Wars and played a major role in the conflict. On August 10, 1512, the *Mary Rose* led an attack on the French at Brest in Brittany. Over 30 French ships were destroyed in the battle. When Lord Admiral Edward Howard died in 1513, the *Mary Rose* became the flagship of Lord Admiral Thomas Howard, Edward's elder brother and successor.

● *The wreck of the* Mary Rose

Shipwrecked!

In 1545, France, under Francis I, launched an attack on England. About 200 ships entered the Solent channel off the south coast of England. The English fleet was led by the *Mary Rose*. On July 18, 1545, the English engaged the French at Portsmouth. Neither side made any considerable gain. The next day as the *Mary Rose* made its way towards the French fleet, it suddenly toppled and sank. All but 35 men aboard the ship drowned.

The English tried to salvage the wreck in 1545. However, they failed and the Mary Rose lay beneath the water unknown for a couple of centuries. On June 16, 1836, the shipwreck was discovered when a fishing net got caught on it. A diver named John Deane recovered timber, guns andlongbows from the wreck. The Mary Rose was once again forgotten when Deane stopped his work in 1840. Later in 1979, the Mary Rose Trust was formed to recover the wreck. The wreck was first lifted close to the water surface using a lifting frame. It was then placed on a support cradle. On October 11, 1982, the wreck was lifted out of the water and placed on dry land. In 1994, work to restore the wreck began. Many valuable artifacts including navigational equipment, guns, arrows, longbows, cooking utensils, board games and musical instruments were recovered from the wreck.

Henry was buried in the St. George's Chapel in the Windsor Castle next to his wife Jane Seymour

King Henry VIII died on January 28, 1547, at the Palace of Whitehall. Henry was succeeded by his nine-year-old son, Edward VI. In just eleven years following Henry's death all his children ascended the throne of England.

Death of a king

In later years Henry had become overweight. This increase in weight was due to a jousting accident in which Henry suffered a severe thigh wound that prevented him from exercising. Moreover, Henry loved to eat and could not resist good food. This added to his problems. Later in life, the thigh wound became infected causing the king more problems and eventually leading to his death.

Edward named Lady Jane Grey as his successor to prevent his Catholic sister, Mary from coming to power

The new king

The Act of Succession of 1544 had proclaimed Edward Henry's immediate successor. Edward therefore became the next king of England although he was only nine years old. In his will, Henry had appointed a council of 16 members to rule on behalf of Edward until the boy king came of age. Edward Seymour, the Earl of Hertford was made the Lord Protector. Edward VI was the first Protestant to rule England.

ELIZABETH I • (September 7, 1533-March 23, 1603) • November 17, 1558 – Became queen of England • 1559 – Elizabethan Religious Settlement • 1588 – Defeat of the Spanish Armada

38 39

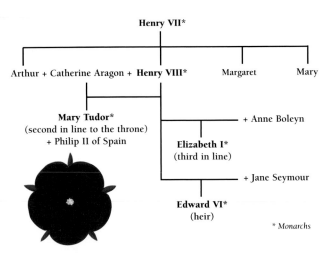

```
                        Henry VII*
       ┌──────────────────┬──────────────┬─────────┐
Arthur + Catherine Aragon + Henry VIII*    Margaret    Mary
              ┌───────────┴─────────┐
         Mary Tudor*              + Anne Boleyn
    (second in line to the throne)
      + Philip II of Spain        Elizabeth I*
                                   (third in line)

                                 + Jane Seymour

                                  Edward VI*
                                    (heir)
                                            * Monarchs
```

🌸 *The successors of King Henry VIII. All of his children ruled England within 11 years of his death*

The next in line

At first, Henry had declared his daughters, Mary and Elizabeth, illegal. However, his sixth wife Katherine Parr helped to bring the king and his daughters back together again. She also convinced Henry to include them in the line of succession after Edward. Accordingly, Mary came to power after Edward died at the age of 15, while Elizabeth succeeded Mary who died childless. Elizabeth never married and therefore was the last Tudor to sit on the throne of England.

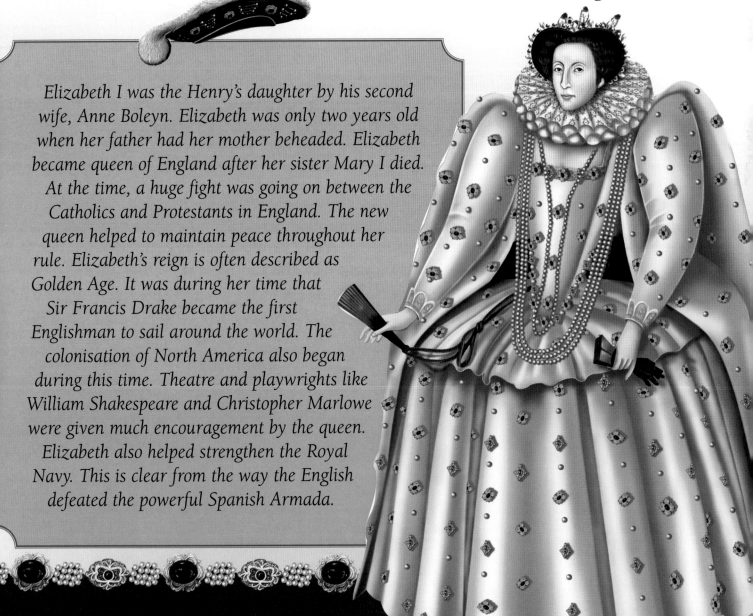

Elizabeth I was the Henry's daughter by his second wife, Anne Boleyn. Elizabeth was only two years old when her father had her mother beheaded. Elizabeth became queen of England after her sister Mary I died. At the time, a huge fight was going on between the Catholics and Protestants in England. The new queen helped to maintain peace throughout her rule. Elizabeth's reign is often described as Golden Age. It was during her time that Sir Francis Drake became the first Englishman to sail around the world. The colonisation of North America also began during this time. Theatre and playwrights like William Shakespeare and Christopher Marlowe were given much encouragement by the queen. Elizabeth also helped strengthen the Royal Navy. This is clear from the way the English defeated the powerful Spanish Armada.

When King Henry VIII came to power people expected a great deal of him. Although he did not live up to most of these expectations, England made immense progress under him. However, Henry is most-remembered for his many marriages than for any of his achievements.

Religious chaos

Henry left behind a lot of religious confusion. Being a devout Catholic, Henry never really embraced Protestantism in his personal life. It was his desire for a son that prompted the king to break away from Rome. Even then Henry did not want to change the Church of England completely. He tried to retain some of the Catholic principles through the Six Articles of 1539, resulting in a lot of confusion that was settled only during the rule of his daughter, Elizabeth I.

● *Henry personally supervised the fortification of the Dover Castle in Kent*

Poor economy

Henry's religious reforms and desire to become the most powerful European ruler led to many wars. By declaring the Church of England independent of Rome, Henry invited the anger of many European rulers of the time, including the Holy Roman Emperor, Charles V. The threat of invasion made Henry spend a lot of money in strengthening the Royal Navy and fortifying England's borders. This left the country in a poor economic condition.

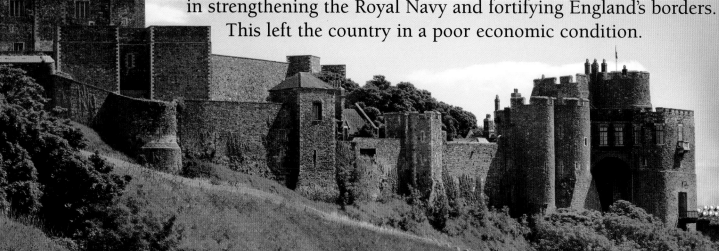

Main achievements

Henry's rule might have been dominated by wars and the king's six marriages, but no one can deny the progress made during his time. He was responsible for uniting England and Wales and thereby improving the administration of Wales. He also made Ireland a kingdom and declared England an empire. However, it was always Henry's personal life that received much attention. A number of plays and films have been made on this subject.

● *The Six Articles of 1539 supported the practice of some Catholic principles, such as confession to a priest*

● *A poster of the film* The Private Life of Henry VIII

Henry in Fiction
Television:
The Six Wives of Henry VIII –
BBC (6-part series)
Henry VIII – *(Channel 4 documentary)*

Film:
The Private Life of Henry VIII *(1933)*
A Man for all Seasons *(1966)*
Anne of the Thousand Days *(1969)*
Carry on Henry *(1970)*
The Six Wives of Henry VIII *(1972)*

Plays:
Henry VIII – *William Shakespeare*
Sir Thomas More – *Anthony Munday and Henry Chettle*
A Man for all Seasons – *Robert Bolt*

LONDON FILMS
PRESENT
Charles
LAUGHTON
IN
The Private Life of
HENRY VIII
DIRECTED BY
ALEXANDER KORDA

Released thru
UNITED
ARTISTS

Timeline

JUNE 28, 1491	*Henry VIII is born*
1502	*Prince Arthur, Henry's elder brother dies*
APRIL 22, 1509	*Henry VIII becomes king at the age of 17 following the death of his father, Henry VII*
JUNE 11, 1509	*Marries Catherine of Aragon in the private chapel of Placentia at Greenwich*
JUNE 24, 1509	*Coronation of Henry VIII at the Westminster Abbey*
1513	*The English defeat the Scots at Battle of Flodden Field. King James IV of Scotland is killed during the battle*
1515	*Thomas Wolsey is appointed Lord Chancellor*
1516	*Catherine gives birth to Mary*
1517	*Martin Luther accuses the Roman Catholic Church of corruption*
1520	*Henry meets King Francis I of France at the Field of Cloth of Gold*
1530	*Wolsey is accused of treason, but he dies on his way to the trial*
JANUARY 25, 1533	*Henry marries Anne Boleyn and is excommunicated by the pope*
JUNE 1, 1533	*Anne Boleyn is crowned the new queen of England*
SEPTEMBER 7, 1533	*Anne Boleyn gives birth to Elizabeth, future queen of England*
1534	*Act of Supremacy is passed making Henry Head of the Church of England*
1535	*Sir Thomas More is executed for refusing to accept Henry as the head of the Church of England*
1536	*Anne Boleyn is executed on charges of witchcraft and treachery*

MAY 30, 1536	*Henry marries Jane Seymour*
1536	*Act of Union is passed making Wales a part of England. The dissolution of monasteries also begin the same year*
OCTOBER 12, 1537	*Queen Jane gives birth to Henry's only son, Edward*
OCTOBER 24, 1537	*Queen Jane dies*
JANUARY 6, 1540	*Henry marries Anne of Cleves*
JULY 9, 1540	*Divorces Anne of Cleves*
JULY 28, 1540	*Henry marries Catherine Howard*
FEBRUARY 13, 1542	*Catherine Howard is executed for treason*
JULY 12, 1543	*Henry marries Katherine Parr*
JANUARY 28, 1547	*Henry VIII dies leaving the throne to his nine-year-old son Edward*

Glossary

Abandon – *Forsake; walk out on*
Appetite – *Hunger*
Assert – *Emphasise; be firm*
Banquet – *Feast*
Beatify – *Bless; sanctify*
Chaos – *Confusion; disorder*
Circumnavigate – *Go around*
Conflict – *Fight; disagreement*
Conspirator – *One who conspires, or plans; schemer*
Convince – *Persuade; talk into*
Coronation – *Crowning*
Criticise – *To evaluate; assess*
Depose – *Overthrow; topple*
Excommunicate – *To exclude a person from the Church, or any other religion*
Execute – *Put to death*
Feud – *Dispute; quarrel*

Heresy – *Dissent; deny the authority of the Roman Catholic Church*
Humiliating – *Disgraceful*
Intensify – *Increase*
Joust – *A combat between two armoured knights on horseback, galloping towards each other with lances*

Maritime – *Naval*
Mercenary – *A foreigner hired to serve in an army; a person who fights for monetary gains*
Oust – *Remove*
Papal bull – *A charter or order issued by the Pope*
Patronage – *Sponsorship*

Portcullis – *Iron or wooden grills at a castle entrance*
Reconciled – *Made peace; arrived at an agreement*
Reform – *Improvement; change for the better; progress*
Ruthless – *Merciless; brutal*
Successor – *Heir; descendant*
Survey – *Study; review*
Tactic – *Plan; strategy*
Treachery – *Betrayal*
Treason – *Deception*
Turmoil – *Disorder; unrest*
Welsh Marches – *Borderlands between England and Wales*